The Passion

The
Passion

Marcus Hummon
and *Becca Stevens*

Church Publishing
NEW YORK

Unless otherwise noted, the Scripture quotations contained herein are from the New Revised Standard Version Bible, copyright © 1989 by the Division of Christian Education of the National Council of Churches of Christ in the U.S.A. Used by permission. All rights reserved.

"Cowboy Take Me Away," text © Martie McGuire and Marcus Hummon, 1999. Used by permission of Hal Leonard.

Church Publishing
19 East 34th Street
New York, NY 10016
www.churchpublishing.org

Cover art: *Blue Jesus* by Marcus Hummon
Cover design by Jennifer Kopec, 2Pug Design
Typeset by PerfecType, Nashville, Tennessee

Library of Congress Cataloging-in-Publication Data
Names: Hummon, Marcus, author. | Stevens, Becca, 1963- author.
Title: The Passion / Marcus Hummon and Becca Stevens.
Description: New York : Church Publishing, 2017.
Identifiers: LCCN 2016040238 | ISBN 9780819233295 (pbk.) |
   ISBN 9780819233301 (ebook)
Subjects: LCSH: Jesus Christ--Passion--Meditations. | Jesus
   Christ--Passion--Biblical teaching. | Passion music.
Classification: LCC BT431.3 .H857 2017 | DDC 232.96--dc23 LC record
available at https://lccn.loc.gov/2016040238

Printed in Canada

Contents

Introduction

When I was commissioned by Christ Church Cathedral here in Nashville to write a cantata reflecting the last days of Jesus's life, I wasn't sure how to begin. First of all, my background is not in sacred music, but rather in popular country music. It just happens that while writing songs for the Dixie Chicks, Tim McGraw, Rascal Flatts, and others, I had started to dabble in writing music for the theater. As I wasn't classically trained, I would need help from a friend of mine, David John Madore at the Hartt Conservatory of Music in Hartford, Connecticut, in transcribing the choral work I was arranging, and my friend Dr. Deen Entzminger and the Belmont Chamber Singers to bring the work to fruition, to full performance. I also asked Jonathan Yudkin to add his beautiful cello accompaniment. Still, I love new challenges in composition and was eager to try my hand at a very different style of vocal ensemble work. Previously, this obsession had led to writing several musicals and an opera, *Surrender Road.* which premiered with the Nashville Opera Company in 2007.

After some research I found that many composers had written cantatas around the passion of Christ; J. S. Bach wrote three! I wondered what I had to offer to this tradition. Selfishly, I wanted a reason to go back and read my Bible, as I had not done any serious study of biblical passages in a long time. Like many churchgoers, my connection to the Bible is the weekly passages from the lectionary. (Lectionaries are cycles of designated readings from Scripture, intended to cover much of the sacred story over a period of time. For Episcopalians, that sequence is three years and includes passages from the Hebrew Scriptures, the Psalms, and the New Testament, particularly the Gospels.)

It was my wife, Becca Stevens, the Episcopal chaplain at Vanderbilt University, who had originally suggested that I tackle the annual Palm Sunday service, where parishioners are often chosen to portray characters in the Passion narrative, and the congregation offers lines spoken by the crowd: "Crucify him! Crucify him!" I felt it would be a great joy to envelop myself in the Lord's final journey to Jerusalem, and see if I could find a musical language for these well-known events to create a unified musical composition. It felt like a wonderful opportunity to dig deep into the texts, and to meditate more fully on my Christian life.

I grew up in the Christian faith; my mom and dad were raised Methodist in small towns in Michigan and Ohio respectively. They eventually swung between the Episcopal Church and the Presbyterian Church, primarily based on their feelings about particular pastors. My father's work was with the US State

Department in economic development and so much of my youth was spent living abroad in Tanzania, Nigeria, the Philippines, Saudi Arabia, and Italy. Overseas, we often had limited choices as to where we could worship as a family.

In Saudi Arabia, for example, we were not officially allowed to have Christian services in the Kingdom, but in the interest of good relations with the United States in the late 1970s, the era of President Jimmy Carter and the Camp David accords, the royal family made an exception for the American business and diplomatic community. Therefore, all Christians who wanted to worship on Sundays in the Saudi capital, Riyadh, were herded into a large auditorium, regardless of whether we were Catholic, Protestant, or Greek Orthodox. Itinerant preachers of a variety of institutional and theological perspectives appeared throughout the liturgical calendar. Every week, it seemed, we listened to a new preacher. And so we all were trapped as it were; Episcopalians sitting with born-again Southern Baptists, Catholics sitting with Mennonites, Nazarenes with Methodists, etc.

There were some pretty lively dialogues in our Christian education classes, but this hardship brought about my somewhat universalist perspective. We really didn't have the opportunity to argue about the manner of baptism, or the proper method of taking communion, or the centrality of the sermon versus the Mass, and the like. The conversation and the focus varied from week to week, and in order to function as a community, it was necessary to develop an appreciation of other Christian walks.

In addition to this, my folks were adamant that I show respect for our theocratic host nation's religion of Islam. My parents, though Christian, firmly believed that God must be working in the lives of Muslims, and by extension, those of other faiths as well. My mother even chose to study Arabic during our two-year tour of duty in Riyadh, Saudi Arabia.

This was a formative period for me in my faith. To move through the *suqs*, or marketplaces, and about the mosques and hear the muezzin prayer call five times a day had a profound effect on me. When I subsequently left home for my sophomore year in high school, options were limited and I enrolled in Notre Dame High School in Rome, Italy. In my homesickness I turned to my faith, and started going to daily chapel, and taking communion with my Catholic classmates. This was not acceptable, and I was brought before the headmaster, where it was explained to me that only confirmed Catholics could take communion at a Catholic Mass at chapel. I said they'd have to expel me, as I fully intended to take communion. I am not sure why, but they decided to let me stay and do as I felt called to do.

Regularly I would take a bus into the city, and enjoy walking the colonnade at St. Peter's, imagining how the Eternal City may have looked to St. Peter and St. Paul, not long after Christ's death. One particularly memorable evening, as I walked about St. Peter's Square, there was an art exhibit by the great Russian painter Marc Chagall; choral music was in the air. I remember inspiration washing over me; a Protestant, in Catholic Rome, far from family in Islamic Saudi Arabia, reveling in the work of a great Jewish artist!

We are all "children of the story." I like to think of the Christian story in broad strokes. A poor Palestinian Jewish preacher emerges at a violent time in Judea, under the brutal tether of the Roman Empire. He preaches a revolutionary understanding of God's love, an understanding that seems to transcend class, wealth, gender, nationality; certainly it transcends all hierarchy and power structures. It is a teaching largely directed at the desperately poor, and it is this teaching that ultimately threatens not just the local religious authority, but more significantly threatens the Romans occupying the Holy Land. This is what finally leads to Jesus's death. The Romans crucify Jesus: a horrific, barbaric form of execution. Still, according to Jesus's followers, three days after his death and entombment, he rises from the grave, is resurrected, and seen by his disciples, just as Jesus is said to have predicted.

Elton John was once quoted as saying, "When in doubt, write a hymn."[1] For a songwriter, these are words to live by. What is a hymn after all, but a musical offering directed at the object of our deepest passions? A hymn can be a lament, a cry, a shout for joy, or exultation—a hymn is a love song!

Most of my adult life has been spent writing love songs. In the world of songwriting, the vast majority of songs written in popular music are love songs in one form or another. And so, I looked at writing this "Passion" as a love song to Jesus. Jesus's story is my story. It is the tale I have been told again and again from as far back as I can remember. It is my heritage and my family heirloom. I cannot think of a nobler, more divine soul than

1. Elizabeth J. Rosenthal, *His Song: The Musical Journey of Elton John* (New York: Watson-Guptill Publications, 2001), 133.

the Jesus I have grown to love. Given the opportunity to set a chapter of his story to music, I decided to jump in!

And as for the question of whether or not I should write a new cantata, on a subject that has been so beautifully rendered by no less than J. S. Bach and so many other great composers, I am reminded of a beautiful passage from the first chapter of Ecclesiastes:

> All streams run to the sea,
>   but the sea is not full;
> to the place where the streams flow,
>   there they continue to flow.

I am simply offering another small stream to the Sea, knowing that the Sea is never full!
Marcus

— *I Come to Jerusalem!* —

When they had come near Jerusalem and had reached Bethphage, at the Mount of Olives, Jesus sent two disciples, saying to them, "Go into the village ahead of you, and immediately you will find a donkey tied, and a colt with her; untie them and bring them to me. If anyone says anything to you, just say this, 'The Lord needs them.' And he will send them immediately." This took place to fulfill what had been spoken through the prophet, saying,

> "Tell the daughter of Zion,
> Look, your king is coming to you,
> humble, and mounted on a donkey,
> and on a colt, the foal of a donkey."

The disciples went and did as Jesus had directed them; they brought the donkey and the colt, and put their cloaks on them, and he sat on them. [8] A very large crowd spread their cloaks on the road, and others cut branches

from the trees and spread them on the road. The crowds
that went ahead of him and that followed were shouting,

> "Hosanna to the Son of David!
> Blessed is the one who comes in the name
>   of the Lord!
> Hosanna in the highest heaven!"

When he entered Jerusalem, the whole city was in turmoil, asking, "Who is this?"
(Matthew 21:1–10)

I Come to Jerusalem

I come not to destroy the law
I come to fulfill the scriptures
To proclaim the acceptable day of the Lord.

I have come to free the captives
To feed the hungry, clothe the naked
I have come to bring long-delayed justice to the poor.

I come to Jerusalem
He comes to Jerusalem
Go tell the daughter of Zion
Look, your king is coming to you
Humble, mounted as foretold,
Upon a colt—a donkey's foal.

Hosanna to the King,
Hosanna to the House of David
Hail the Messiah
Blessed is he who comes in the name of the Lord.

Hallelujah, hallelujah, hallelujah, hallelujah

O my Jerusalem, I weep for thee
City that kills the prophets
and stones the messengers of our God.

Hosanna to the King,
Hosanna to the House of David
Hail the Messiah
Blessed is he who comes in the name of the Lord.

Hallelujah, hallelujah, hallelujah, hallelujah

Even rocks and stones shall sing Hosanna to the King

I come to Jerusalem!

Becca

I learned in seminary that there are five kinds of prayer: lament, praise, adoration, intercession, and confession. I also learned that all five of those forms of prayers can be found throughout the one hundred fifty Psalms. Each psalm can be divided into one of those themes and it is a way of seeing the whole range of emotions the psalmists experienced. Sometimes they were writing from the mountaintop and experiencing God in the holy dwelling place. Sometimes they were in the valley feeling the loss of love. Other times they were in the fields teaching the wisdom of the ages to the next generation. Marcus's composition based on Jesus's entry into Jerusalem reminds me that those five types of prayers can also be found bundled together in one event. That we can wail as lamenters over the state of violence, injustice, and cruelty at the same time we are singing in adoration over the sunrise. We can praise God in worship with hands held high while we plead for mercy on behalf of a sister who is suffering. We can beat our chests and beg for mercy as we weep, grateful that we feel Love so close. All of those prayers live together in our hearts and when we allow ourselves the gift of faith, they come out together in words and deeds and even songs. We feel it all. We rejoice, we grieve, we hope. Faith cannot always be dissected into five distinct parts. It's a living entity that imbues our experiences with a multitude of feelings.

The passages in Matthew record the humble and glorious entry into Jerusalem and hold those prayers in perfect tension. Jesus explains his instructions for how it will unfold at the beginning of the twenty-first chapter. He is fulfilling an old prophecy and instructing his disciples on how to carry it out. Marcus's melodies and orchestration add drama and power to the spoken word. The music helps conjure up for me the vision of how costly and lonely it can be to live into our truth. The disciples knew the cost of entering Jerusalem and what was coming. The occupied nation was one that killed its prophets and shut down rebellions. They must have felt both great anticipation and fear at the same time. They were participating in watching Jesus begin that humble journey on a donkey that would usher in the events that would lead to his violent murder. But along with those divergent feelings was this overwhelming joy and adoration as the crowd sings "Hosanna in the highest" and lays down the branches. The Scriptures record that the whole city was in turmoil, so the praise must have been almost at a frenzied level. The entry into Jerusalem is filled with layers and layers of feelings and it is only in song that such depth and breadth of emotions can be expressed. We wail and sing, lay branches and raise our arms as we feel the adoration and longing that live within all of us.

Beyond that, the music invites us to contemplate how we are living into our truth. In other words, where are we in this passage? Are we laying down branches we have cut and joining the crowds? Are we singing praise in the streets for all the mercy we have known? Are we ready to stake our lives for the sake of truth as well? Do we even know what we believe or what we would sing? We are called through the Passion narrative to ask the question again, "Who is this man?" Such a question is central to our lives of faith and how we will live into our faith. Jesus rode into Jerusalem on a donkey and received a king's welcome. He was a force that inspired men and women to lay down their lives. It was a radical act that leaves us—no matter how many times we have heard the story—wondering again, "Who is this man?" How can we worship him with our whole hearts?

Jesus has been making his way to Jerusalem for three years. His whole ministry happened as he and his friends made their way to the Holy City. It begins after his baptism by John and his retreat to the wilderness. There he learns about his strengths and temptations. There he wrestles with the beasts and is tended by angels. In the wilderness he begins his journey to Jerusalem. What could have been a two-week trek for him and his disciples took him his whole life as a rabbi to make. He was sidetracked by the suffering he encountered "on the way." He was delayed by the needs of a community that entreated him. He was backtracking for friends who were ill and imprisoned. Along the way he is teaching and preaching about the acts of mercy required and what to expect when he gets to the gates of Jerusalem. It's a journey that prepares the community and the disciples' hearts for what love requires. He teaches the disciples that healing is possible, and then he keeps walking toward the city that will kill him. It is a beautifully sad and dramatic story of what love looks like in flesh and bone.

—

The question this music and the passage ask us to reflect upon is simply: How close to Jerusalem are we? Are we ready to lay down our cloaks, to be at a place where the rocks and stones shout "Hosanna," and to answer the questions about whose we are? Are we still near Galilee on a hillside eating a piece of bread from a basket and trying to figure out where it came from? Are we at a place as communities of faith and individuals to risk more so that we are proclaiming the gospel in a way that is worthy of the Passion? The Passion is the climax of the story and the journey to Jerusalem doesn't make sense without it. Without the Passion, the journey through the wilderness loses both its tenderness and depth.

It is a gift to wander in the wilderness and explore our faith. That is a necessary part of the journey. To contemplate in silence, always ready to listen to new ideas is a great way to be a student of faith. But faith also requires action of us. Faith asks us to take a stance and be on the side of love. There comes a time when we have to enter the gates and to be ready to sing "Hosanna in the highest" and lay down our branches and say, "Yes, Lord, we believe."

For me, the transition from the wilderness to Jerusalem happens as Jesus weeps in the garden. Those tears feel like they were formed in him during his whole three years in the wilderness and through the cities. They were forming as he encountered the suffering of the people he came to serve and in the face of the injustices he had to confront. Even though he was strong when John was killed or when the women anointed him with oil, the tears must have been there. Those tears are also an expression of the longing he feels for what we could be and what the kingdom could look like. It doesn't have to be a world that kills its prophets or rejects its children. When Jesus weeps over the city before he enters, it feels like one of the most intimate and honest moments of the Gospels. The tears offer us a glimpse into the heart of God. As a pastor, I see over and over how grief puts us on the hard and holy ground where we are asked to dig deeper into our faith and find out what we really believe. It is where our faith is not tested, but fired like iron and made strong.

We are called to remember that in the life of faith, it's not just the journey; it is the destination. We are heading to Jerusalem, where we will weep and praise and adore and lament. We will be asked, "Do you know him?" "Did you see him in the homeless person you passed by today?" "Did you see him in the widow's offering?" In the Passion, the destination is close by. We feel the tears closer and the need to sing praise. The Passion is at the heart of our faith and as we reenact it every year, it is an invitation to remember our destination. It is not just a beautiful piece of music, a historical reenactment; it is a calling to remember our own destination.

This morning I went outside and felt the sunrise like warm wine on the back of my throat. I saw two beautiful rabbits feasting in Marcus and my overgrown yard where clover is abundant. I felt a cool breeze kiss my cheek in the midst of a hot summer morning. I felt the space rising in my soul to sing praise to our Lord and to birth new ideas. Time was as expansive as the sky. This morning I could have been at the gates of Jerusalem. I could easily have laid down my cloak in gratitude and sung, "Alleluia! Praise God from whom all blessings flow." I could have kissed Jesus's feet and waved a palm branch.

Aaah, but not yesterday—yesterday there was another mass shooting in America, there was relapse after nine long months by a woman I have been working with, who has survived rape and being shot by her pimp, and there was a storm that hid the sunrise. Yesterday I felt anxiety about death and had to visit three people sick in the hospital. Yesterday one of our almost-adult children had a party to watch a sports event and I felt suspicious.

Yesterday Marcus was visiting his parents who are nearing their own deaths. Yesterday was hard. What I need to learn on those days is that there, too, I am close to the gates of Jerusalem. There, too, I can sing "Alleluia" even as I weep.

So how close to Jerusalem are we? My bet is that we are closer than we think. The wilderness is not that far from the gates. The distance between here and there is a walk. The space between wandering and coming home is smaller than our fears lead us to believe. The difference between being a spectator and participant is as small as a bended knee. The pilgrims are closer to the heart of God than they know. To be close to Jerusalem—a metaphor for coming to the heart of our faith—means three things:

We are prepared to surrender control for love's sake.

We are prepared to speak our truth.

We are prepared to confront powers and principalities with that truth and love.

These are huge idealistic steps that we practice taking, even as we are sitting outside the gates. They are steps that help us discern where we are and what we need to let go to pass through those gates. In Marcus's *Passion*, we can feel the drama rising as Jesus prepares for all three consequences of being close to Jerusalem. We put ourselves into the midst of that drama and find out where we are in the story so that it takes on new life in us.

———

For reflection, reread the first ten verses of the twenty-first chapter of Matthew and consider the following questions for the beginning of the Passion narrative.

Given that this first part of the Passion places us right at the gates of Jerusalem, and those gates represent the transition from wilderness to Jerusalem:

- How has your faith community prepared you to be at the gates of Jerusalem?
- How has your faith community prepared itself to be at the gates of Jerusalem?
- How has your faith community prepared the wider world to be at the gates of Jerusalem?

Marcus

As I consider the journey of writing this cantata, I am reminded of the words attributed to Martin Mull: "Writing about music is like dancing about architecture."

Like most folks who call themselves Christians, I do not consider myself a theologian. Until writing this cantata, I had never done a serious study of the passion of Christ; I felt I knew the story. I imagine that most church-going Christians don't have, or don't take, the time to really dig into the various Gospel accounts of the end of Jesus's life. In composing *The Passion*, I chose to create five musical segments for soloists, choir, and piano (and percussive hand-clapping). The five segments reflect Jesus's final days in Jerusalem: his entrance into the Holy City, his last meal with his disciples and final teachings, his arrest on the Mount of Olives, his trials, and his crucifixion. I chose to precede each of the five musical offerings with a reading from one of the Gospels corresponding to the events musicalized, and found myself using different Gospel accounts from one piece to the next; that is, unlike other composers, I didn't limit myself to one Gospel (e.g., Bach's *Passion According to Matthew*). In fact, with the readings and with the libretto itself, I moved from one Gospel to another, picking and choosing my favorite passages, and sprinkling in Hebrew Bible texts where they either emerged as part of the Gospel accounts, or where they seemed to surface from my own consciousness: a limited, yet not empty reservoir of biblical passages. It seemed an authentic way to approach this creative process; I think this is how many of us read the Bible today.

Also, I realized that, despite my assertion that most of us are not theologians, when it came time to choose passages for the musical libretto, it is actually the case that all of us who call ourselves Christians are at least armchair theologians. Choices have to be made.

In the first piece, "I Come to Jerusalem," I found myself especially appreciating Matthew's account of Jesus's entrance into the Holy City. Like the crowd, I found myself wondering aloud: "Who is this?"[2]

"Who is this man?" felt like the overriding theme of the moment. Jesus comes to Jerusalem, on this most holy of occasions, to celebrate Passover with his disciples, to preach and to heal. There would have been a large ragtag crowd of followers at

---

2. Matthew 21:10

his side. Word of mouth about the healings and miracles would have been spreading for some time, along with the growing claims of the coming of a Messiah as promised by the prophets.

Jesus enters humbly, on a colt and not a war horse, and Matthew tells us that this was foretold by the prophet Zechariah:

> O daughter Jerusalem! Lo, your king comes to you; triumphant and victorious is he, humble and riding on a donkey. (Zechariah 9:9)

I begin the cantata with Jesus's voice alone, proclaiming his vision. His opening a capella pronouncement is a series of quotes combined to form a proclamation, beginning with the words of Matthew 5:17: "Do not think that I have come to abolish the law or the prophets; I have come not to abolish but to fulfill."

Jesus has made a point to enter Jerusalem humbly, yet certainly he can hear the shouts of "Hosanna" and "Son of David." He would have known that many in the throngs surrounding him would be expecting a worldly king, a warlord, someone who might free them after years of tyrannical occupation at the hands of Rome. It must have been a wondrous sight!

The joyous harmonies, counterpoint work, and the use of the text from Isaiah are meant to evoke the excitement and cacophony of Jesus's entrance through the gates. It is meant to arouse in the listener the joy of the moment.

And then I found myself moving to Luke's account.

Luke tells us Jesus was still for a moment, as emotions overcame him:

"As he came near and saw the city, he wept over it."[3]

Luke gives us clues into Jesus's life and heart, but it is a profound image that defies simple explanation. I imagine Jesus is contemplating the violent past of the Holy City, as well as the probable violence ahead; that his coming to Jerusalem will almost certainly end in his torture and death. I like to think that his weeping is a sign of tenderness for humanity's brokenness and folly. Perhaps it is also a foreshadowing of words Jesus will speak, forgiving his tormentors on the cross.

"Forgive them, for they do not know what they are doing."[4]

The truth is, we don't know what Jesus was thinking. I've learned in my years as a performing songwriter that sometimes the power of an image is the way that it can transform, change, evolve, live, and take on different shapes in the human heart.

Years ago I wrote a song with Martie McGuire of the Dixie Chicks called "Cowboy Take Me Away." She wanted to write a song for her sister's wedding, and her sister was marrying a cowboy: a country singer who had a ranch and broke horses. Martie had the title and the beginning of an arpeggio on mandolin. I had the start of a lyric about freedom, and returning to simplicity and nature.

I want to touch the earth
I want to break it in my hands
I want to grow something wild, and unruly.

3. Luke 19:41
4. Luke 23:34

We found our two paths toward the song, met in a beautiful place, and we finished the song in a matter of minutes. Martie and Natalie sang it for Emily at her wedding with Charlie. Later, it was chosen to be the second single on the Chick's top-selling album *Fly* and became a hit on country radio.

Consequently, over the next few years I found myself playing the song at festivals and songwriter nights. At one such night I was part of a fundraiser held at The Bluebird Café in support of cancer research St. Jude Children's Hospital. There were several patients and survivors with their parents, and as I played the song I could feel many reactions to it. There were tears on several faces, especially the face of a little girl sitting near me as I performed. When the show was over, this little girl with a scarf covering her head came up to me and said, "'Cowboy Take Me Away' is my favorite song and the Dixie Chicks are my favorite group!"

"I love the Chicks as well!" I agreed.

She continued, "I was wondering about something. The words in the chorus say:

Cowboy take me away,
Fly this girl as high as you can into the wild blue
Set me free, O, I pray,
Closer to heaven above, and closer to you
Closer to you.

"What I was wondering is the 'cowboy' in the song, is that God? Did you mean that the cowboy is really God?"

I thought about how Martie and I had come at the song from different vantage points and that the central image of the song probably had very different meanings for each of us. I took a breath and told the young girl that her vision of our song was as beautiful as the song itself, if not more beautiful. And yes, the "cowboy" in the song was, indeed, God.

So given the power of Luke's image of Jesus stopping the procession to rest quietly with his own thoughts and weep, I decided to create a musical break in the movement, taking the piece out of tempo, and changing the time signature, creating a moment where Jesus sings what might be described as a soliloquy, or an "aside" to the listener. He steps away from the crowd and offers us an intimate insight into his interior world.

"O my Jerusalem, I weep for thee . . ."

Musically, however, we cannot stop; the moment passes, and Jesus moves forward through the gates of holy Jerusalem. For a moment, all is right in the world. The four-part harmonies return, ushering Jesus into the city and then seem to multiply with the addition of hand clapping and Jesus's voice hovering above! The Messiah has indeed come, "gentle, riding on a donkey" as foretold. We hear the cries of "Hosanna to the King," and "Blessed is he who comes in the name of the Lord." Jesus steps into the vortex of this Passover, surrounded by the hopes and dreams of freedom. He is also surrounded by those who feel threatened by his vision, his proclamation of love and justice, and the power and the authority that must have accompanied the sound of his voice.

"I come to Jerusalem!"

— In Remembrance of Me —

Then came the day of Unleavened Bread, on which the Passover lamb had to be sacrificed. So Jesus sent Peter and John, saying, "Go and prepare the Passover meal for us that we may eat it." They asked him, "Where do you want us to make preparations for it?" "Listen," he said to them, "when you have entered the city, a man carrying a jar of water will meet you; follow him into the house he enters and say to the owner of the house, 'The teacher asks you, "Where is the guest room, where I may eat the Passover with my disciples?"'" He will show you a large room upstairs, already furnished. Make preparations for us there." So they went and found everything as he had told them; and they prepared the Passover meal.

When the hour came, he took his place at the table, and the apostles with him. He said to them, "I have eagerly desired to eat this Passover with you before I suffer; for I tell you, I will not eat it until it is fulfilled in the kingdom of God." Then he took a cup, and after giving thanks he said, "Take this and divide it among yourselves; for I tell you that from now on I will not drink of the fruit of the vine until the kingdom of God comes." Then he took a loaf of bread, and when he had given thanks, he broke it and gave it to them, saying, "This is my body, which is given for you. Do this in remembrance of me." And he did the same with the cup after supper, saying, "This cup that is poured out for you is the new covenant in my blood. But see, the one who betrays me is with me, and his hand is on the table. For the Son of Man is going as it has been determined, but woe to that one by whom he is betrayed!" Then they began to ask one another, which one of them it could be who would do this. (Luke 22:7–23)

I am the true vine, and my Father is the vinegrower. He removes every branch in me that bears no fruit. Every branch that bears fruit he prunes to make it bear more fruit. You have already been cleansed by the word that I have spoken to you. Abide in me as I abide in you. Just as the branch cannot bear fruit by itself unless it abides in the vine, neither can you unless you abide in me. I am the vine, you are the branches. Those who abide in me and I in them bear much fruit, because apart from me you can do nothing. Whoever does not abide in me is thrown away like a branch and withers; such branches are gathered, thrown into the fire, and burned. If you abide in me, and my words abide in you, ask for whatever you wish, and it will be done for you. My Father is glorified by this, that you bear much fruit and become my disciples. As the Father has loved me, so I have loved you; abide in my love. (John 15:1–9)

In Remembrance of Me

Blessed are the poor in spirit
He said blessed are they who mourn
Blessed are the meek for theirs is the kingdom of God,
    for they shall be comforted
Blessed are they who hunger for righteousness,
    for they shall be satisfied.

This is the bread of the new world to come
This is my body, broken for you
Do this for me, in remembrance of me.

He said blessed are the merciful, blessed are the
    peacemakers
Blessed are those persecuted for my sake,
    blessed are the pure in heart
I remember what he said.

This is the wine of the new world to come,
This is my blood which is spilled out for you
Do this for me, in remembrance of me.

Every time you eat the bread, do this
Do this for me, in remembrance of me.

Every time you drink the wine, do this
Do this for me, in remembrance of me.

If ever you betray me, if ever you deny me,
	I forgive you.

If you abide in me as I abide in you
For the branches cannot bear sweet fruit
And are thrown to the fire unless they do
	abide the vine.

I am the vine, you are the branches
And as the Father has loved me so I have loved you.

One last commandment left to do
Love one another as I have loved you.

Every time you eat the bread, do this
Do this for me, in remembrance of me.

Every time you drink the wine, do this
Do this for me, in remembrance of me.

I remember what he said.

Marcus

In thinking of how to approach the Last Supper, I wanted to compose around the language of communion, of the bread and wine. But as I compared each Gospel account, I realized that John's account doesn't include a communion feast nor the words of blessing and sacrifice that have become the central feature of the Christian communion liturgy for two millennia. Instead, in John's Gospel, there is a lengthy set of teachings that scholars have come to call the "Farewell Discourse." Included in John's account is the moment where Jesus says he has one more teaching for his disciples, that he wants them to love one another, just as he has loved each of them. Well, as this call to love is central to my own faith in Jesus, I wanted to keep both of these traditions—the teaching and the meal—and just weave them together.

I began to think about these two strands and what they have in common. In both cases, it seems very important to Jesus that his words be remembered!

"Do this in remembrance of me."

When someone dear to us dies, we find ourselves reminiscing about the times we had together. We cling to those last fleeting moments, bitter and sweet. The death of Jesus would have been a traumatic moment for his community of followers, and would have imprinted in their hearts the indelible mark of his teachings. They would recall his final words, and repeat them to one another. We do not know much of the life of the early Church, but we do know of the practice of commemorating the life of Jesus with a communal meal blessed with words that evolved into the liturgies in which we participate today. The disciples repeated this memorable, final repast with their Lord.

I began "In Remembrance of Me" with a somber tone, as a chant in which the Beatitudes are sung, the phrases weaving together, and ending with the refrain,

"I remember what he said."

Our memories are immortality itself. To be remembered is to be loved, to be remembered is to have lived.

Recently I have been visiting my parents who, in their mid-80s, have had various health challenges. My mother's memory has been failing for years due to progressive dementia. I have watched my mom courageously trying to hang on to her memories and to her sense of "present" reality, even as she seems to drift into the past through the photos and newspaper clippings she stares at as if they were speaking to her. As a memory comes clear to her, she writes a note to herself, to remind herself in the coming days of a moment of illumination.

She is also a musician, and a true lover of music. Both my parents are musicians: they met in choir at Albion College in Michigan. Mom loves all types of music and helped to encourage an appreciation in her children for all the arts, but especially music. She has followed my career very closely through the years and keeps boxes of clippings and other memorabilia.

As her ability to remember declines, she spends more and more time playing the grand piano in her home. She reads and plays beautifully, with the expression of an artist, full of emotion and shifts in dynamics. In her present condition, however, she plays the same few songs over and over again. One of the songs she plays is a tune I cowrote, "Bless the Broken Road," a song recorded by several artists but most notably by the country pop trio Rascal Flatts.

During one recent visit she seemed distant and sad, and went to the piano to play her usual assortment of tunes. She played for twenty minutes or so, with the lights off. While she was playing

"Bless the Broken Road," I joined her at the piano and asked if she'd mind if I played the song. She smiled and seemed amused as she rose from the piano bench.

I sat down and played the piano part as I played it when we wrote it over twenty years ago. I played it as I have countless times. I played it as mom had heard me play it a thousand times. As I moved through the piece, playing it by heart and singing, a glow appeared on my mother's face.

"Did you write that?" she asked, clearly surprised.

"Yes, mom, I did write this one!"

"Oh, that is beautiful!" she exclaimed, and as she said these words, I could see on her face that a huge wave of memories was washing over her and she was experiencing years of shared joy, remembering not one song, but hundreds of songs. I knew in that moment we could see each other clearly, and that music and poetry were a bridge to a lifetime of love.

— —

And so we move solemnly from the opening chant of this piece of music into the language from the Eucharist that many of us know from the depths of our own memories. "This is my body broken for you, this is my blood spilled for you." In the cantata, Jesus and the disciples sing, "Do this for me, in remembrance of me," as if it were a repeating chorus, they sing it together, in four-part harmony. One of the things that stands out in many songs is the chorus. It is always easier to remember a song's chorus—or at least, it should be. The Last Supper is the night that Jesus wants to be sure that his disciples know the lyrics and the chorus to his life's song.

I also wrote these familiar liturgical lines as a waltz because of the intimacy of the moment. Although Jesus is restating themes he has preached throughout his ministry with his disciples at his side, he is not shouting from a boat on the Sea of Galilee now, nor projecting to a crowd on a hillside. He is speaking softly, almost in a whisper, encircled by his dearest friends and followers. This, to me, is a kind of dance, and the "one-two-three, one-two-three" cadence of a waltz seems appropriate.

Midway through the serene waltz of Jesus's sacrificial blessing, I inserted the rest of the Beatitudes, as yet another important sermonic recollection, and the repeating phrase,

"I remember what he said."

Jesus must have known that his time was short, and it appears from the Gospel accounts that he had become aware of Judas's treachery. He could intuit the possibility of Peter and others denying their discipleship in the face of a brutal purging on the part of the Romans. All of this might well have filled Jesus's heart, and he would have been moved to offer himself and his mission of love one last time in a sacramental manner.

My task as composer, then, became to merge the music of the familiar liturgical language taken from Matthew, Mark, and Luke's Gospels with John's vision of Jesus's final thoughts. I created a musical "hinge," where Jesus sees the betrayal and the denials ahead and forgives all in advance, as long as, "If ever you betray me, if ever you deny . . . know that I . . . forgive you . . . if you . . ."

With these words you can feel the music shifting out of the waltz rhythm, beginning to slow down, and finally coming to a complete stop. I move the music into a new meter or cadence, to a new place harmonically, and shift to the Johannine language of poetry and metaphor. That is to say, we hear new melodic strains above a slow count of four, not three, as in the waltz. The melody is related to the earlier chorus of "Do this in remembrance of me," but it also evolves in a new way, as Jesus offers a new teaching to his disciples:

> Abide in me, as I abide in you. Just as the branch cannot bear fruit by itself unless it abides in the vine, neither can you unless you abide in me. . . . Whoever does not abide in me is thrown away like a branch and withers; such branches are gathered, thrown into the fire, and burned. (John 15:4, 6)

He continues on, interpreting his own metaphor, telling his disciples that he is the vine, and that they are the branches, and to stay close to him, for as the Father has loved him, so he has loved the disciples. At this point, Jesus winds down toward what sounds to me like a good-bye, with the familiar and beloved admonition. For this, I created a musical breakdown, so that I could underscore the emotion of this moment. As Jesus finishes singing the words, "So I have loved you," I bring the music to a halt, as if Jesus is measuring the impact of this last thought. After a moment of reflection, Jesus decides to press home the point:

> I give you a new commandment, that you love one another. (John 13:34)

As a composer, I can take some liberties in order to musically and dramatically shine a light on a particular verse, and so I repeat Jesus's words,

"Love one another, love one another . . ."

And then again, dramatically, with the disciples creating echoes around this most beautiful phrase, as if they fully grasp his teaching,

"Love one another. Just as I have loved you!"

I think it is clear from the Gospel of Luke, the book of Acts, and Paul's letters that many of the first-century followers of Jesus believed that the end of days were upon them, and saw in Jesus's brutal crucifixion the onset of the apocalypse.

However, I doubt that Jesus saw it in this way. Rather, I think Jesus really did want to give his disciples a new commandment for the difficult times ahead; he knew that without radical love for one another, without redemptive love, without the love expressed in the Beatitudes, without the love pictured in the parables, without the love of the Sermon on the Mount, without the love that rejected the stoning of a prostitute, without the love of mud and spittle opening the eyes of the blind, without a healing love—without a love like this, life falls short of its full stretch, and human freedom and joy are unattainable.

He bade them to "remember" all of this: for the journey ahead, for the days, years, and the centuries ahead!

"I remember what he said."

Becca

Communion is the sacred meal. It is the ritual that binds Christian communities as one. It is considered the foretaste of the heavenly banquet that we share with the cloud of all the saints who have shared the bread and cup since the Last Supper. The rituals of our eucharistic meal are some of the oldest rites we have. The theology and practice of communion has defined Christian identity and communities for the entire history of the Church. At the heart of communion lives the possibility that we can move beyond the political and economic barriers that keep us separate. There is the hope that in communion we can all be served at one table and become one body. Although the practice of communion differs among denominations, the hope of communion remains the same; that we come to the table for solace, strength, pardon, and renewal. That the grace of the Holy Communion makes us closer to one another and to the heart of God. Communion is the meal that forms us and forms our communities in a spirit of humility and gratitude.

Marcus's words and music give new life and possibility to the old words. The second section of *The Passion* cantata offers breadth and depth to the old and intrinsic knowledge we inherited through the ritualized breaking of the bread and sharing of the cup. We are invited into the intimacy of the disciple's meal with their rabbi. We are invited to see the disciples like Da Vinci's painting, close together and engaging one another, alive and full of individual thoughts as well as a collective spirit, sitting at a table preparing for the Passover meal. We can sense the wonder and feel the anticipation as the bread is broken in the tender music and whispered memories. We know our own ritualized meal by heart and so it is a gift that through this music we are invited to hear the old words again and feel them taking on new life in us. In most communities we have eaten loaves of bread one bite at a time and consumed a gallon of wine one sip at a time. This is an invitation to taste and drink another bite and sip with new life. To take in something we may have forgotten and remember what draws us to that Holy Table in the first place.

Listen again to this piece and hear the disciples echoing, "I remember what he said." By tying in the words from the Sermon on the Mount into the ritual of communion, Marcus is binding the beginning and ending of Christ's teaching into a continuous and seamless piece. He is speaking to the very pulse of what makes us Christian. Remembering who we are and what the founding principles he laid out for his community are is central to accepting bread and wine as holy and life-giving sacraments. Communion is the culmination of our life of faith together. It is the place we go— whether we stand or kneel around the altar—that holds memory.

Memory is part of why communion is so powerful. It is not hard to imagine that as Jesus said the words, "Do this in remembrance of me," all the disciples began to recall the lessons that Jesus taught them along the way. As he was breaking bread and saying "This is my body," they could recollect their first encounters with him and all the moments when he was teaching them about love. As he was pouring the wine and saying "this is my blood," images of him on the water at dawn or in the mountains on retreat must have flooded their thoughts as they tried to remember everything he was saying. It is a holy thing to remember, and it fills us with new meaning and hope.

Communion is the holy moment when we feel the thin veil between life and death tear in two. Communion has history, theology, and practice so deeply woven into the simple act that sometimes it is hard to remember the essence of its holiness. There are tomes written about it. There are rubrics that define how we hold our hands, lay the towel down, and bow when we say certain words. There are even gates, ambos, and cathedrals designed to keep us segregated from the elements offered in communion. Such architectural, liturgical, and historical barriers make remembering more important. We remember that Jesus and his disciples were sitting together, knowing the end was coming soon, and broke bread. So as we listen to this piece and remember, the first question that rises in me is, "What do we remember? What lessons did you learn at a communion when you were young? What moments stand out as lessons of grace? Do you recall a time when communion felt particularly healing?" Those are all questions about remembering. They invite us to add deeper meaning to our communion by remembering all the communions that have come before. Those remembrances are the key to finding the treasured needles in the haystack of possible meaning in eating bread and drinking wine. They bless the bread broken for us and allow it to feed our hearts. Those remembrances make the wine rich with fragrances of loved ones who have died and temples where we have worshipped over the years.

As one who has served communion thousands of times, my memories flow like a river. I remember seeing blisters, tattoos, and

scars on hands held up to receive a piece of bread. I remember
seeing the light dancing off the host and weeping at the beauty of
it all. I remember trying to make our children behave at the altar
and looking over at Marcus with gratitude that he was keeping
them every Sunday morning while I tried to focus on the words
of the Last Supper.

As I listened to Marcus's music, I felt weepy, because I
remembered my mother's last communion. We were in a small
circle on a Wednesday evening. The tradition in the little chapel
where I have served for more than twenty years is that during
weeknight services each person in the circle offers communion to
the person on their left. My mom turned to the right to receive
communion and then tried to turn left to offer communion to
the next person, but her balance was off and she started to fall
over. The people around her broke circle and held her up as she
finished passing the cup. She never came back to church and died
at home from a brain disease within a couple of months. While
that feels so stark to write, the truth is there is so much gratitude
and tenderness in the memory. The Passion and the Last Supper
are linked by death and the promise that we can still remember and live in hope. Without the crucifixion, the Last Supper
is just another Passover. Without the drama of death, there is no
Passion. When Jesus says, "Remember me," it is powerful because
we know his murder is imminent. His words take on a weight
and the music lives somewhere between a requiem and resurrection mass. It lives in the fragile space.

We know as communities of faith that the communion circle, like the Last Supper, contains brokenness as well as promise.

It is right that the words change from remembrance to forgiveness of one another. In this act Jesus knows that as we remember, we also need to forgive. The dance between remembering and forgiving allows healing and grace. Remembering and forgiving are linked throughout Scripture as Jesus reminds us that we can go in peace; our sins are forgiven. They are linked in all the healing stories that lead up to this Last Supper and they are linked in our own lives. There is really no eucharistic feast if there is not also pardon and renewal. The Book of Common Prayer teaches us we don't come for solace only, but for strength. Then we pray that the grace of the communion gives us a renewed sense of how to serve the world in Christ's name. Forgiveness is the element that transforms the brokenness of remembrance into compassion for others so healing is possible. That is the formula offered by our Lord to the community and it is sung with grace through this piece of music that pierces the heart.

To prepare for this reflection, you are invited to read the Beatitudes from Matthew 5:1–12 and then to read the accounting of the Last Supper in Luke 22:7–37. Read these two together and pay attention to the memories that rise in you. Have you heard the Beatitudes read at weddings or funerals? Do you have a special Scripture that you recall when you listen to the words of communion? Do you have rituals in your practice of communion that link remembering and forgiving? Do you know the prayers of the Eucharist by heart? Does that make them more meaningful, or less?

— The Kiss —

Then Jesus went with them to a place called Gethsemane; and he said to his disciples, "Sit here while I go over there and pray." He took with him Peter and the two sons of Zebedee, and began to be grieved and agitated. Then he said to them, "I am deeply grieved, even to death; remain here, and stay awake with me." And going a little farther, he threw himself on the ground and prayed, "My Father, if it is possible, let this cup pass from me; yet not what I want but what you want." Then he came to the disciples and found them sleeping; and he said to Peter, "So, could you not stay awake with me one hour? Stay awake and pray that you may not come into the time of trial; the spirit indeed is willing, but the flesh is weak." Again he went away for the second time and prayed, "My Father, if this cannot pass unless I drink it, your will be done." Again he came and found them sleeping, for their eyes were heavy. So leaving them again, he went away and prayed for the third time, saying the same words. Then he came to the disciples and said to them, "Are you still sleeping and taking your rest? See, the hour is at hand, and the Son of Man is betrayed into the hands of sinners." (Matthew 26:36–45)

The Kiss

This is the rising of the moon
Behind the branches of the olive trees
Our eyes grow weary with the end of day
But keep the vigil we must try to, try to stay awake—

And so we pray,
Behold my servant in whom I uphold
This is my elect in whom my soul delights.

A bruised reed he will not break
A dimly burning wick he will not blow out—

I was not there when he walked on the water.
I was not there when he turned water to wine.
But I was condemned to die living on the streets
And he was the first man to ever offer me
The kiss of peace, God's peace
He said "Rise up child and sin no more!
    I do not judge thee."

Will no one stay awake with me here in this
    time of trial?
Will no one wait and watch with me here
    in this time of trial?

Lord, if this cup could pass from my lips,
    then let it be so.

Will no one stay awake with me here in
    this time of trial?
The spirit is oh so willing, but the body is oh so weak.
Lord, if this cup could pass from my lips,
    then let it be so,
But not my will, Lord, let it be yours and yours alone.

He will not give you any trouble
He surrounds himself with fools and dreamers,
    hangers-on
I should know because I once was first among
    his throng
Can you imagine this? Arrest the man I kiss.

What's the use of a messiah who won't raise his sword?
Yet allows the women to anoint his feet with
    precious oil—
Saying "there will be poor always" while he enjoys
Luxuries like this—arrest the man I kiss.

Judas, would you betray me with a kiss?

Becca

A secret garden is the place we go to be with our hearts as we long for solitude or to grieve. A garden is a place of sanctuary and it is the perfect setting for the third part of *The Passion* cantata.

Finding ourselves alone with Jesus, we pause a minute in the midst of all the public activity and drama to feel what must be on his heart as he contemplates the next steps. Within that safe garden space, we are given a glimpse of the juxtaposition of weariness and watchfulness within the unfolding passion. Through the powerful words and haunting music, our imaginations are stirred so that we can feel a bit of his pain as we come to terms with the realization that what love requires is heartbreaking. The scene in the garden offers us a glimpse into a moment of truth and surrender Jesus has to face alone. The disciples can't do this for him, or even with him. The women who have walked with him have not come into this space. It is a reminder that "take up your cross and follow me" is a calling we have to answer alone, no matter who may be walking beside us as we bear it.

The Gospels teach us that Jesus knew this day was coming. He knew that it was the consequence of facing the religious authority, challenging the occupiers, and confronting old biases. He knew that Jerusalem was a city that killed its prophets; he had been threatened with death already. Yet he kept going. He kept healing on the Sabbath, loving women others saw as unclean, and cleaning out the temple. He picked up his cross, not on the road to Golgotha, not here in this garden, but when he said, "Love your enemies," and called his disciples to go out on the mission to love. This time in the garden, then, is the realization and reckoning of all he has done, surrendering to the full consequences of loving this world. The Garden of Gethsemane is the place Jesus understands what it is he has lived for and how to accept where living for love has led him.

The question that arises, then, from the garden is how we respond to the calling of Jesus to pick up our cross and follow him. Taking up our crosses and following Jesus is not a call for us to ask what we are willing to die for, it is asking us what we are willing to live for. What will we do with our days and years to live for love, so that when we sit in our Garden of Gethsemane and do our own reconciling—while we may still weep and wish the cup would pass us by—we will know we lived for love? How do we surrender to love? How do we bear the burden of love so completely that it demands we confront powers and principalities and has consequences?

It was a revelation to me as I listened to the cantata that the kiss of betrayal took place in the same garden where the disciples had been sleeping and where Jesus was grieving even to the point of death. That the betrayal occurred in so intimate a setting becomes even more heartbreaking as we contemplate again the events of the Passion. Jesus's acceptance of that betrayal and the moment of his conversation with Judas should break our hearts. It is a reminder of the brokenness of this world. That we are called to keep loving and forgiving after such a betrayal seems almost impossible, yet that is where we find the very heart of God.

I met a woman named Regina when I founded Thistle Farms twenty years ago. She was living on the streets after experiencing much trauma in her youth. She was a survivor of addiction, prostitution, and trafficking. She was the mother of three young boys. She was the first woman I met through this community who began to teach me in small and profound ways that you can't kill hope in people. You can betray them, you can jail them, and you can assault them, but you can't kill the hope and the deepest parts of their hearts. In 1997, shortly after we opened the first house, I stopped by and saw her dancing in the window. When I came in and asked her why she was dancing, she said she was having a Holy Ghost party. We laughed and when I went back to my car, I sat for a while, crying. That was one of my Gethsemane moments. It was the setting for the realization and reckoning I needed to be ready to take up my cross. I cried because I wanted to believe that in spite of all the pain and brokenness in this world, love is more powerful and forgiveness runs deeper. I cried because I knew this work was going to take up so much of my life, and I cried because I couldn't remember a time I had danced with the Holy Spirit. Regina helped lead me to that space. She went on to help another two hundred women come off the streets and now is one of the national education directors for sister communities. For a couple of years she helped Marcus and me raise our three young sons. She is a teacher who helped us find a way to take up our cross and follow love. I am so grateful to her.

— · —

In reflecting on this passage, it would be helpful to read Matthew 26 again and put all the sequence of events in place. It is significant to remember how Jesus and the disciples get from the Last Supper to the arrest. To see how they find their way late at night to the garden where the betrayal will take place. After rereading this section, the most basic question to ask yourself is where is your Gethsemane? What does your cross feel like? Have you come to accept the reckoning that you are blessed to bear even though it is costly? In my reckoning I believe that there is less pain in bearing our crosses for the sake of love than in not knowing love at all. There is less pain. The vision I have of the disciples as they slept and dreamt in Gethsemane is that they too were reckoning. They had taken up a cross and left everything to follow Jesus. They knew imprisonment and maybe death awaited them. The burden was huge and they were buckling under its weight and had to sleep for a bit. But when they awoke, in spite of the great cost, the deepest feeling was gratitude. Gratitude that they were present to see the feeding of the five thousand, to see the lame walk and the blind see. Gratitude that they broke bread with the Messiah, the holy One, and feel the love of God beside them. They awoke ready to defend, ready to serve, and even though they would continue to stumble under the weight of their own crosses, they would continue to follow love's path all the way to their own deaths.

The lesson is clear: taking up our crosses and following Jesus is not about carrying around an undue burden like a ball and chain. It is the opportunity to define what our lives stand for and what our legacy will be. Carrying our crosses is a journey blessed with gratitude—and even joy. If what you define as your cross does not have gratitude and joy, you should cut off that ball and chain, because bearing a cross is about freedom as much as it is about duty. In our lives of service to one another and devotion to God, there must be tears not only of grief, but of unbounded joy for the love we have known and the hope we have been given. It is not in spite of the betrayal and death that we are called to love each other with our whole hearts; it is because of that betrayal and death.

We get to live for love. That is why even in the garden the cry is both a lament and a prayer of thanksgiving. We get to take some time and do a bit of reckoning. My hope and prayer conjured up by the soulful melodies Marcus offers is that we don't let the cup pass us by. The question for discussion may be too private, too close to the heart to answer in a community. Gethsemane is a private time, between us and our beloved Creator who sits with us. What we can do for one another is to do our best to stay close by, and to wake up when we are called to listen and bear witness. Taking time to pray and write in silence as a community is powerful. So take some time, and do some reckoning as we live into our passion.

Marcus

Jesus and his disciples, both men and women, escape the weight of the crowds and the tension that is building around them to find a place to rest for the evening. They retreat beneath the shade of olive branches, just outside the city walls, to the Garden of Gethsemane. We must imagine that his inner circle is exhausted by the pace of Jesus's ministry and their own attempts to keep their Lord moving, out of danger.

Now they have come to lay their heads down and rest. Though they must have had private thoughts at this time of the evening, they are unified in their desire for rest, and so I begin with tight harmony, sung almost as a lullaby. They sing about exhaustion, about eyes grown weary, and yet there is a vigil to be kept, for danger surrounds them and threatens their Lord. In an attempt to stay awake, they recite the well-known passage from Isaiah where the coming of the Messiah is prophesied. In the musical setting, I chose to have each choral voice holding a single note in harmony against the changing chords beneath the words of Isaiah; this nonmelodic approach creates a kind of prayerful chant, emphasizing their shared belief that they are following the Messiah foretold by the Prophet.

"Here is my servant, whom I uphold, my chosen, in whom my soul delights."[5]

As if in answer to the yearning belief that Jesus is indeed the Messiah foretold, a single voice emerges above the choral chanting, a woman singing of her experience with Jesus. This solo voice rises as if to give testimony to the truth of Jesus's divinity. She is the woman, often understood as a prostitute, who was to be stoned, whom Jesus protected with the admonition,

"Let anyone among you who is without sin be the first to throw a stone at her."[6]

The woman sings of her life as an outcast, of living on the streets, and of what it meant to have Jesus intercede on her behalf:

"He was the first man to ever offer the kiss of peace, God's peace."

I imagine the woman about to be stoned, taking Jesus's hand once those who would have stoned her to death have retreated. As Jesus encourages her to "go and sin no more," I see him leaning in to kiss her on her forehead. It is a kiss of innocence reclaimed.

---

5. Isaiah 42:1
6. John 8:7

As the soloist reaches a crescendo with her telling of Jesus's promise that he does not judge her, the choral parts begin to swell beneath her voice, and both musical strands intersect with the choir confessing:

"I believe he is the Chosen One."

Despite the disciples' efforts to stay awake, we are told by the Gospel writers that Jesus is left to stand vigil on his own; although perhaps one of his intimates was awake long enough to hear the Lord's voice as he prayed aloud:

"Will no one stay awake with me?"

For this sad and exquisitely beautiful chapter in the passion of Christ, I wrote this as a waltz, rising and falling with Jesus's internal dialogue, his prayers, his fears, and his ultimate submission to the will of God. As in the previous piece, "In Remembrance of Me," the use of the waltz cadence brings about the intimacy of a dance, and what could be more intimate than overhearing Jesus's prayers and private thoughts? In one of the most memorably human moments in the Gospels, we hear Jesus express loneliness, and even fear for the coming violent ordeal. Musically I began each of two stanzas with a melody of entreaty directed at his disciples, a plea for companionship in this dark moment. The second movement within each stanza is an ascending melody, directed toward his Father in heaven, asking that he be spared the terrible ordeal that awaits him. We listen to Jesus in this passage, as a theater audience listens to a Shakespearian soliloquy, and follow his prayerful monologue, as Jesus reaches a conclusion, choosing to submit to the will of God:

". . . but not my will, Lord, let it be yours and yours alone."

What stands out to me is that Jesus seems to know what is about to happen. He has asked not to be handed over to suffering, but he knows what's coming and wants the closeness of friends before he is apprehended. Jesus knows what will happen because he knows how cruel and unjust the world is: he has seen a crowd ready to stone a woman to death; he has been face-to-face with the hypocrisy of authority figures; he must have seen his share of Roman brutality, perhaps crucified bodies lining the roads, a method of execution commonly used by the Romans to warn against rebellion.

The loss of innocence can weigh heavily on us all.

My first experience of cruelty and violence was 1971 while my father was posted in Lagos, Nigeria, working for USAID. We lived in a beautiful home with a gun-toting guard at the gate, a nanny, a cook, a driver, and a gardener. In 1971, Nigeria had just ended a terribly bloody civil war, which began when the predominantly Igbo tribe in the northeast of Nigeria had seceded and formed the state of Biafra in 1967. Over the next three years of military conflict, over a million souls perished in the oil-rich Biafran state before its eventual capitulation.

All this was just a lot of talk as we sped along the Nigerian coastline in a speed boat driven by my Boy Scout leader. I was a Webelos scout, only eleven years old and in pursuit of a fishing badge. We slowed the engines along Bar Beach and set trolling lines in the water. Before long my line was singing and I was straining to reel in a young barracuda.

"Keep your line tight, no slack or he'll get free!" yelled my scout leader.

He had turned off the motor for the angling fight and the boat drifted toward shore. As the barracuda began to tire and slice slowly near the boat, I noticed there was blood in the water—a lot of blood. We all seemed to see it at once. The boat had drifted dangerously close to the shore and there on the beach was a huge crowd, hundreds and hundreds of people straining to view something. As my scout master cursed under his breath and began to reverse engines, my eyes became accustomed to the sight and I suddenly realized what everyone was looking at. There were four large oil cans tied to poles dug deep into the very edge of the surf. Strapped with wire to each of the oil cans were seemingly lifeless bodies, bleeding into the surf, leaning and drooping against the wire. Up the beach were soldiers with machine guns, and behind them, the great circus of a crowd.

I remember trembling with fear and shock, as the captain walked up to each body and delivered the "thud" of a bullet into the head of each prisoner, the crowd cheering. The young barracuda thumped lifeless against the boat, still on my treble-hooked line, as we retreated to deeper waters.

After this experience I began to know the cruel absurdity of the world. I have had many experiences of human evil and brutality, but that was when I first knew. Jesus knew all too well what was coming, and must have wondered if it was worth staying the course and accepting the savagery ahead.

Reflecting on this memory of mine, I see the loss of innocence of a young boy. Every loss of innocence is a kind of betrayal. However, I see Jesus in the Garden of Gethsemane as innocence reclaimed. Yes, Jesus knew the world, and knew what pain and degradation awaited him, but he stepped forward anyway. The betrayal and horror of the moment were not allowed to diminish the ministry of love.

— —

The final section of "The Kiss" is meant to have a certain dissonance. In order to do this, I set the section apart, and without any specific time signature or consistent rhythm. Just when you hear a phrase expressed in what may appear to be a meter (a certain pattern of stressed and unstressed beats), the next phrase is shaped differently. We are not allowed the comfort of repetition here. The piano score sets notes in close proximity together, and not in familiar thirds or fifths. To the ear, it sounds like a child simply placing his hands on the piano and pressing keys clumsily. The effect is slightly disturbing, nonmelodic, and almost atonal. I am attempting to express in musical terms the dissonance of Judas's betrayal of Jesus. Judas leads the Roman authorities to Jesus to arrest him, and we hear Judas commenting derisively that Jesus is a "lamb" who will not resist, that Jesus is surrounded by "fools and dreamers," and even admits, with chagrin, having once been "first" among this company.

Then as Judas and the Roman authorities approach Jesus, the two voices and the sentiments they are expressing overlap, allowing Jesus and Judas to sing in duet.

"What's the use of a messiah who won't raise his sword . . .," Judas asks.

Jesus exhorts the disciples to respond nonviolently, "Put your sword back into its place."[7]

An angry Judas continues, recalling Jesus's allowing the women to anoint his feet with precious funeral oils, ". . . and allows the women to anoint his feet with precious oil, saying, 'You will always have the poor with you, but you do not always have me.'?"[8]

This intertwining duet continues until they converge on the word "kiss."

Judas says, "The one I will kiss is the man; arrest him."[9]

Jesus says sorrowfully, "Judas, is it with a kiss that you are betraying the Son of Man?"[10]

This is what has come to be known as the "kiss of death": Judas's kiss of deep brokenness that precedes his treachery. This musical moment is meant to be juxtaposed with the earlier reference to a kiss, Jesus's kiss of peace, sung by our soloist, the woman Jesus saved from being stoned. As the music singles out this tragic last confrontation between the two men (who must have traveled together, and perhaps were once dear friends), I cannot help but make this moment musically gentle and bittersweet with a final arpeggio in a minor key. We cannot see into the heart of Jesus at this juncture, but I imagine that he felt empathy for Judas, for all human frailty, and perhaps Jesus is already forgiving Judas in this moment, even as Judas condemns himself.

---

7. Matthew 26:52–54
8. John 12:3
9. Matthew 26:48
10. Luke 22:48

— Wherever I Am —

As soon as it was morning, the chief priests held a consultation with the elders and scribes and the whole council. They bound Jesus, led him away, and handed him over to Pilate. Pilate asked him, "Are you the King of the Jews?" He answered him, "You say so." Then the chief priests accused him of many things. Pilate asked him again, "Have you no answer? See how many charges they bring against you." But Jesus made no further reply, so that Pilate was amazed. Now at the festival he used to release a prisoner for them, anyone for whom they asked. Now a man called Barabbas was in prison with the rebels who had committed murder during the insurrection. So the crowd came and began to ask Pilate to do for them according to his custom. Then he answered them, "Do you want me to release for you the King of the Jews?" For he realized that it was out of jealousy that the chief priests had handed him over. But the chief priests stirred up the crowd to have him release Barabbas for them instead. Pilate spoke to them again,

"Then what do you wish me to do with the man you call the King of the Jews?" They shouted back, "Crucify him!" (Mark 15:1–13)

Wherever I Am

Wherever I am, I am walking in Galilee
Along the Sea of Galilee, wherever I am.

Oh they say that you have walked on water
They say that you have raised the dead
Strange you bleed like any other man
when we strip you, whip you, and place thorns upon
    your head.

Wherever I am, I am facing the holy city
The holy city on bended knee, wherever I am.

Well, they say you are a king, a king of what?
A kingdom where? In Judea Caesar reigns—
Well, they say you are the chosen one, the messiah
Where is your army? Israel is in chains—

Wherever I am, I am singing songs of joy
    and adoration
Ballads to the author of creation! Wherever I am!

Crucify him, you must crucify him!

I tell you, I could not sleep at all last night
This man came into my dream.

What manner of man is this who can lift
    the veil of night
What kind of sorcery?

I will break this fool upon a tree
So all can see what happens to the enemies of Rome
I will wash my hands and put an end to revolution
Two birds, one stone.

Wherever I am, I am loving you with all my spirit
With all my spirit, body, and soul,
    with all my suffering, flesh and bone, wherever I am!
Wherever I am, I am loving you.

Marcus

In this piece, I wanted to pull together the varying descriptions offered in the four Gospels of Jesus's arrest and torture, humiliation, and trial, incorporating images of the crown of thorns, the whipping, the interrogation by Jewish authorities, and, finally, Pontius Pilate.

I decided to create a forward-leaning vocal and piano "pulse": my left hand playing open fifths, not betraying a major or minor chord setting, all set against the rhythm of my right hand tapping on the piano, pushing the music forward, just as Jesus would have been pushed from one brutal and humiliating episode to the next. Without committing to a major third or a minor third in my left hand, I do not determine the emotional context of each interrogation, but rather a sense of movement from one location to another. It is as if this musical piece is a "montage" in cinematic terms, moving through fast edits of each interrogation, and in and out of Jesus's consciousness. To enhance this, I have the male ensemble vocals mirroring the left hand pulse, as if they were a double bass playing along with the piano. Above this pulse we hear the voices of interrogations, voices intent upon humiliating Jesus and trying to coax him into blasphemous statements. In response to each of these pulsing segments, I decided to do all I could to move inside Jesus's spirit.

In the synoptic tradition (the Gospels of Mark, Matthew, and Luke), Jesus is all but silent during his interrogation and torture. His seeming unwillingness to cooperate or to legitimize the brutality and duplicity that confronted him only served to infuriate his captors, and may have ultimately sealed his fate. Where was Jesus's mind and spirit during this ordeal?

I imagine Jesus's silence as song:

"Wherever I am, I am walking, along the Sea of Galilee . . . wherever I am! Wherever I am, I am singing songs of love and adorations, ballads to the author of creation . . . wherever I am!"

— — —

My musical journey has led me to writing for the theater and my latest work focuses on the life of the abolitionist, writer, and statesman Frederick Douglass. I have adapted his first autobiography, *Narrative of the Life of Frederick Douglass: An American Slave*, published in 1845, seven years after Douglass escaped from slavery and bondage in Maryland. My piece is a concert-theatrical, weaving narrative, scene work, songs, instrumentals, dance, and choral music. In writing the music and the choral arrangements for *Frederick Douglass: The Making of an American Prophet*, I have been influenced by Nashville's own Fisk Jubilee Singers and their director, Paul Kwami.

The Jubilee Singers have been keeping the spiritual alive since 1867. As I sit in the Fisk University Chapel and watch the dozen men and women standing tall and straight, elegantly dressed and singing the songs of slaves, the voices seem other-wordly. It has been said that the spiritual was a kind of soulful deception: that the songs seem to speak of yearning for heaven, and yet in truth, these are songs of yearning for freedom.

"Swing low, sweet chariot, coming for to carry me home."

"Home" is freedom, or a free state, and the chariot may well be the Underground Railroad.

Frederick Douglass speaks of slaves singing in his first auto-biography, noting not just the slave masters' inability to compre-hend the true meaning of slave songs, but the deafness displayed by those Americans who lived in the Northern Free states.

I have been utterly astonished, since I came to the north, to find people who could speak of the singing among slaves as evidence of their contentment and happiness. . . .

The songs of the slaves represent the sorrows of his heart; and he is relieved by them only as an aching heart is relieved by tears. At least, such is my experience. I have often sung to drown my sorrows.[11]

And so I imagine Jesus sings in his spirit to relieve his aching heart. He sings of love, and fearlessly sings of freedom. Even as he is bound and beaten, he imagines walking along his beloved Sea of Galilee. When we hear Jesus's voice within this song, the feel of the music shifts from the pulsing interrogations to a melodic arpeggio, and ultimately to a defiant chorus.

"Wherever I am, wherever I am!"

As the music and the stakes rise, so too does the intensity of Jesus's rich interior life: his abiding faith in the Father, his unwillingness to turn his back on his ministry, his call for coming of the kingdom, despite the obvious threat before him. I see Jesus's relative silence before his tormentors as a kind of waking prayer; and so, as Pilate makes the final decision to crucify him, Jesus's final lines in the libretto for "Wherever I Am" are:

"Wherever I am, I am loving you, with all my spirit, body and soul, with all my heart, flesh and bone, wherever I am!"

This is Jesus's insistence that God is with him, and he is with God, and "nothing" and "no one" can separate us from the love of God! This is also the faith that I, as composer and as an individual, want to convey, and want to experience. I too want to be fearless, I want to be prayerful, I want to be singing for God, wherever I am!

---

11. Frederick Douglass, *Narrative of the Life of Frederick Douglass, an American Slave, Written by Himself*, Bedford Series in History and Culture (New York: Bedford Books, 1993), 47.

Becca

The fourth piece of the cantata moves quickly as the music and the questioning of Jesus intensifies. The scene shows Jesus never wavering in his commitment to love—and then we hear the haunting words "crucify him" coming in at poignant moments. This scene is told in various ways in the different Gospels, placing the blame on the crowds, the Romans, and the religious authority, depending on which Gospel account we read. The words of the crowd, though, remain consistent: "Crucify him."

I think that is where we are intended to find ourselves in the unfolding drama. We are supposed to identify with the throng of people: perhaps the same crowd that ate on the hillside, perhaps the same crowd that laid down the branches at his feet, or perhaps the same crowd that will follow him to Gethsemane. We are the followers of the Holy One and we must come to terms with the reality that we have not lived into our faith, that we have followed the crowds and denied him, and that we have turned against one another. It is our history and it part of human nature to prefer not to stand out and pay the price for speaking up. That is why it is written into the liturgy of our worship. We confess we have sinned against God and our neighbor in thought, word, and deed: "We have not loved you with our whole heart."[12] We confess the doing of things we should not have done and confess

---

12. Episcopal Church, *The Book of Common Prayer and Administration of the Sacraments and Other Rites and Ceremonies of the Church: Together with the Psalter or Psalms of David According to the Use of the Episcopal Church* (New York: Seabury Press, 1979), 360.

the things we should have done that have been left undone. The writers of the Book of Common Prayer were so certain that we would continue to act in this way it became part of our weekly gathering in worship. Those writers didn't even know us and yet they knew that we would need to confess our lack of concern for creation, our love of worldly goods, and our betrayal of those we love.

Given this is the nature of our common life together and the reality of falling short for one another in community, a good place to begin this reflection is to ask ourselves: What is required of us as bystanders to injustice? That is the burning question that haunts me as I hear the trial, torture, and humiliation of Jesus in this part of the Passion narrative. What is required of us as disciples when we witness the mass incarceration of people who are victims of racism, the violence of poverty, and the short side of systemic justice? What does it mean for us to stand quietly on the sidelines because we don't want to "stir the pot" or risk people leaving the church when we call for an end to gun violence or CIA torture? These are not questions that can be answered easily, and they are complicated by the fine line that we draw between our politics and our faith. As a speaker, preacher, fundraiser, and chaplain, I am consistently aware that when I stand in front of a crowd and begin to speak, I am probably either too Christian or not Christian enough for most of the people in the room. That is true for all of us. We want to stay within the norms of our community and not offend, but this Gospel asks us to consider, "At what cost?" At what cost do we keep the peace or keep a silence? When do we know it is time to speak our truth in love, even if it puts us in a more precarious place? I do not believe that the pulpit is the place to lay out our partisan politics, but it is the place to speak against the principalities that refuse to hear the cry of the suffering. As we study the Bible and reflect together on our life as Christians, we need to talk in our communities about gun safety, immigration, women's rights, and all the other topics that tend to divide us. If we don't, we remain complicit in the ongoing suffering in the world around us.

I recently heard about a program in an Episcopal church in Wyoming where the entire season of Lent was spent hosting a conversation seeking common ground on justice issues that affect us all. They took the time and made the commitment to one another to find ways to talk about these difficult topics together, so they could be a better witness in the world around them. I admire that kind of hard work, allowing communities to find their voices to speak up for those who need more advocates in this world.

These passionate questions about our roles in contemporary injustices stir up in us as we engage the story of our Lord's last day in flesh among us. Where were the disciples? Where was Magdalene? Where were the five thousand people he fed a few chapters back?

I am not sure there is such a thing as a Lenten sin, but if the institutional church suffers from one, I believe it is our attempts to manicure the wilderness. We clean it up to make it palatable and safe for people who come and then we lose our relevance. We quit going down to the riverside because the water is muddy. We quit giving away our money because we get scared there won't be more. We create regulations to protect our communities from folks who are homeless and lock our doors to keep ourselves safe. All of these acts and others like them lead us to a sanitized form of faith that keeps the ungainly messiness of this world away from the church and leaves the church without much relevance to the world. The way that I have understood it is that a church without beggars is just a museum. We are the beggars: we are people who have been in the ditch and that have known injustice. We need the church to remember to stand up for us when we are suffering.

I remember our family visiting a church in Rwanda where five thousand people were murdered in 1994 during the genocide. The young man who led the tour told us that people were invited to come and find sanctuary inside when the genocide began. Women, children, husbands, and neighbors gathered inside the tightly packed church. Once they were all amassed, the perpetrators of the horrific crime against humanity came through and killed almost everyone inside with clubs, knives, and simply by swinging small children against the walls. We stood and wept as the guide showed us the stacks and stacks of shoes, bottles, blankets, and bones preserved as a memorial. Then he told us that he had been inside and was the only member of his family to survive. He leads the tours now so that we never forget the story. He wants his family remembered. Again, the question begs to be answered: Where were we? Where was I?

The calling from the Portico in Jerusalem is to speak our truth in love even when our voice shakes. It is to stand up for justice when we are given the chance. Martin Luther King Jr. talked about this when he recounted the story of the Good Samaritan. He said that the question for the Samaritan wasn't what will happen to me if I stop. The question he asked (as opposed to the others who passed by) was: What will happen to him if I don't stop? I believe the question is also: What will happen to me if I don't stop? What will it do to my spirit if I don't stand up for truth and don't live into the justice I long for?

When Jesus answers with silence in this space, I wonder if for a moment the bystanders wanted to yell out, "He is the Messiah, the holy One of God. He is the one who cured my leprosy and told me the truth at the well. He is the one who answered my questions in the dark of night and who went back and healed my brother. He is the one who stopped them from stoning me and the one who saw me in a sycamore tree." But the silence lingered and the drama continued to escalate. We know that it is now written in stone that they are going to kill him. It doesn't make it less heartbreaking.

This section of the cantata should stir up the anger that is a part of our lives of faith. It makes me mad at myself, and makes me sad that our church communities could do more. We could do more to stand in solidarity with those who are suffering; those who know the inside of prison walls and the underside of bridges and the backside of anger. I have a feeling that if I were to imaginatively place myself into this scene, I would be standing on the edges, feeling angry and saying nothing, at least not loud enough for Pilate to hear. Where would you be? Would you be saying "Crucify him"? Would you be in the portico watching and silently weeping at the injustice and cruelty played out before you?

— Outliving the Child —

Two others also, who were criminals, were led away to be put to death with him. When they came to the place that is called The Skull, they crucified Jesus there with the criminals, one on his right and one on his left. Then Jesus said, "Father, forgive them; for they do not know what they are doing." And they cast lots to divide his clothing. And the people stood by, watching; but the leaders scoffed at him, saying, "He saved others; let him save himself if he is the Messiah of God, his chosen one!"

It was now about noon, and darkness came over the whole land until three in the afternoon, while the sun's light failed; and the curtain of the temple was torn in two. Then Jesus, crying with a loud voice, said, "Father, into your hands I commend my spirit." Having said this, he breathed his last. When the centurion saw what had taken place, he praised God and said, "Certainly this man was innocent." And when all the crowds who had gathered there for this spectacle saw what had taken place, they returned home, beating their breasts. But all

his acquaintances, including the women who had followed him from Galilee, stood at a distance, watching
these things. (Luke 23:32–35, 44–49)

Outliving the Child

He will always be young in my eyes
He will always be laughing with friends
Through the fields, climbing trees
Now his beautiful body is broken
The soldiers revile him and I am the saddest of souls,
For I have outlived my child.

Father, forgive them for they know not what they do.
Truly I tell you, tonight we will be in paradise.

Do not sing the songs, do not whisper the prayers
Conjure no healing rain from the dry desert air
Gone is my son's gentle smile, eyes flashing fearless, wild
There is no wonder left in the world,
        for I have outlived my child.

Dear friend come closer—here is your mother now—
Oh, mother, come closer—here is your son now.

I thirst. I am so thirsty.
Father, why have you forsaken me?

Blessed is he who comes in the name of the Lord!

I commend my spirit! It is finished.

Becca

Good Friday; that oxymoronic name for the day Jesus was crucified. It seems impossible that on the day the temple curtain is rent in two, that love incarnate is killed and the hope of the people is snuffed out, the community calls it good. Except that the Gospels are Good News and this is the crowning of goodness. This is not the day that good triumphs evil in my reading; it is the day that love is crowned as holy and life-giving. Good Friday is the day when love doesn't die but is poured out for the world. As Marcus captures the last words of Jesus on the cross, he makes the juxtaposition of the goodness of love and the tragedy of death completely transparent as between each of the phrases we hear the refrain, "Alleluia." So we contemplate good as Jesus proclaims, "I thirst," "Why have you forsaken me," "I commend my spirit," and "It is finished." Each time the beautiful broken voice cries out, we remember that even this is good news. This is the truth for our lives as well. Even in our death, as we make the grave our bed, the liturgy of the church says, we make our song, "Alleluia, alleluia, alleluia." The cross asks us to reexamine what we believe love is and what it looks like. How can we practice unconditional love? Love that keeps loving beyond all the events that transpired during Holy Week and all the events that cause us loss or pain. Love that is beyond the gentle nature described by Paul in that famous passage in his letter to the Corinthians. Unconditional love can be hard and painful. If we are the loving followers of God, then it is not just how we live, but how we are called to die.

I was in Memphis serving a justice tea party to tell the story of Thistle Farms and our efforts to love the world, connecting with social enterprises for women who have survived lives of trafficking, addiction, and devastating poverty all around the world. After the speech, slide show, and toasting, a young woman who had escaped trafficking just six months before in Texas and now living in a sister program of Thistle Farms in Memphis, gave me a hug, "What is unconditional love anyway?" she whispered in my ear as her arms encircled me. That whisper in a crowded, noisy room silenced me. She had made her way across the room with her heart open enough to hear beyond the brokenness and violence that must have filled her life for the past few years. While none of us can answer her question, I believe it is the lesson of the cross that we are to ask each other again and again, "What is love?" So I spent the early morning hours with that question and have tried to write a love letter to God and to her.

Here are three aspects of what I believe "unconditional love" to be and how we are to live it out in our lives. First, unconditional love is truth. Love is woven into the fabric of creation and so it is part of our DNA. We have stardust coursing through our veins, oceans for tears, and love in our very fiber. Love, then, is not a feeling we need to search for, but the truth of our lives that calls us to seek justice, offer mercy, and forgive all that we have done and left undone—and all that has been done and left undone to us. I have seen women forgive more than I thought possible for the sake of love. I have seen women relapse because they couldn't

recognize the truth that they are love. In light of this unconditional love, all the other questions we have asked this Lent make
sense. It makes sense that it took the disciples three years to make
their way to Jerusalem and for us to find our way from wilderness
to the gates. It takes a while to live into the truth of love, preparing our hearts to embrace the whole world. Unconditional love
needs to be nurtured in communion as we remember. It needs to
live beyond betrayal, and thrives in the midst of our trials. The
truth of love makes all the clanging bells ring in harmony in a
graceful melody that it can reach past cynicism, fear, brokenness,
and the sting of death. Love is the truth, my dear sister.

Unconditional love is the root of all faith. There is no faith
outside of love. As Jesus is dying, he reaches out with compassion to his mother and the beloved disciple. He was still loving,
because without love, none of it makes sense. There is so much
injustice experienced by survivors. But if we want to find love, we
can't just rail against principalities; we have to get to the root of it
all. Love that is powerful enough to carry us through this world
demands that we overturn old hard ground in us, that we lift old
stones that prevent growth, and dig deep furrows into our hearts.
There we find love that makes dirt loamy and nourishing so roots
can withstand storms and produce new life.

Unconditional love is our deepest desire. Being in love can
be unfathomable and sometimes seems unattainable, but it is
our deepest hope. On long nights when worries sit by our beds,
on gray days when we wonder how the clock ticks seamlessly as
hours drag on, and on lonely roads when longing overshadows
community, our desire for love does not cease. There is always the

hope of love. After the death and resurrection of Jesus, a community who is still praying, "Lord help my unbelief," gathers. Paul speaks to them of their desire to live into the truth of love. He tells them to remain in fellowship, to live in generosity, and to break bread together. We may never fathom the reality of love requited, but our desire to love well will keep us close to the heart of God. Love does heal us all. Love is not a commodity one person bestows upon another, but a grace that fills us as we live in fellowship, with generosity for all as we break bread.

Love is the truth, the root of all faith, and our deepest desire. It is the key to freedom, the pearl of great price, the one sacrament of the Church, the plowshare made from swords, the measure of our worth, the eternal kiss on our temporal lips, the substance of dreams, and the connection between two strangers. I pray we never stop asking the question or allow the answer to trip us up.

I once led a small funeral for a woman who died in state custody, weighing eighty-five pounds and chained to a bed with a feeding tube. Even as she was dying, when it looked like all the brokenness of the world had landed on her back, she longed to feel love. I don't remember feeling more afraid to preside at a funeral than I did at hers. It seemed like love did not win, that a traumatic youth, a devastating addiction, poverty, and poor choices were more powerful. I feared that maybe we are not capable, that the problems are too big, or that people just die. As a tiny group gathered around her ashes in a cardboard box, we divided the tasks of praying, offering words of comfort, and a song. Before the first line of prayer was uttered, we all began to weep. Love was so thick in the room that words could not cut through it. When there is nothing else, love fills a space. I knew in that room if there was ever a chariot coming for to carry a soul home, it had come for her and carried her to the bosom of her Lord.

Love does have the powerful last word: God does so love the world. If the world can do its worst and still love, unconditionally and lavishly poured out, can speak that loudly, we can gladly lay down our lives for the sake of it. Such love is enough to assure us that we will find our way home and remind us that we were enough all along.

What do you believe unconditional love to be? And, maybe more importantly, how does your life preach that truth? This is where the rubber hits the road; where the hard wood of the cross meets the foundation of the world. All across the world people gather during the week we call holy and on this day we call good, asked to be a living witness to love in light of this most sacred and loving act the world has ever known.

Marcus

The four Gospels have their own distinct accounts of Jesus's final words on the cross. In Matthew's and Mark's accounts, after suffering in silence for hours, Jesus suddenly cries out, "My God, My God, why have you forsaken me?" and dies. Luke and John each offer different versions of Jesus's last words. This becomes a serious issue when trying to choose a libretto for a musical composition based on the Passion.

For hundreds of years, Christians have come to remember the "seven last words" of Jesus, actually seven last phrases, an amalgam of all four Gospel accounts. This has been referred to as "biblical harmonization," a musical metaphor conveying the blending of multiple traditions into one tradition, taking on an almost liturgical significance. With these seven last words of Jesus I had much from which to choose for the libretto of this fifth piece in *The Passion*.

Still I wanted to focus the composition, as I had throughout the cantata, on the humanity of the moment. I found myself looking about the scene of Jesus's crucifixion at all the faces: the disciples, the soldiers, the angry opponents of Jesus, the crowds that have prayed desperately that Jesus is the Messiah foretold and now look on in horror as the subject of their devotion is to be cruelly and humiliatingly executed. Still, in my imagination, as I survey the crowd, the face watching the brutal proceedings that I find myself settling on is Mary, Jesus's mother. We are told that Mary was present, and one can only imagine what might have passed through her mind as she witnessed her son's execution. As any parent knows, our worst fear is outliving our children. It is the ultimate nightmare.

Several years ago, friends of ours lost their little boy in a tragic drowning accident at a neighbor's pool. I will never forget the devastation our friends suffered. My wife, Becca, presided at the funeral and managed somehow to speak to the grief as the congregation sat in a kind of stunned disbelief. In that first year after the child's death, the little boy's father would sometimes stop by our home after work and simply sit in silence on our living room couch. I would sit in silence with him.

So I decided to begin this musical passage a capella, coming out of silence, and written from Mary's perspective, grieving the loss of this most beloved child. I set her lines in a minor key, and operatic in tone and vocal range, to emphasize the depth of her pain. Opera singers generally utilize a much wider vocal range than popular singers do to coincide with the highly dramatic swings within operatic librettos and subject matter. To communicate the wide-ranging emotions of the art form, opera singers are trained to push their voices to the edge of what is possible for the human instrument. Operatic composers are therefore able to employ melodies that stretch well beyond those of most pop music composers.

As Mary looks on in horror, she looks beyond the image of her son, tortured and dying, to the memory of the child, as well as the memory of the beautiful and strong man he grew to be.

"He will always be young in my eyes," she sings.

From Mary's expression of grief, we move back to the cross, and as Jesus speaks we hear the crowd murmuring below, calling out his name. Jesus offers the extraordinary expression of compassion and forgiveness found in Luke's account . . .

"Father forgive them, for they know not what they do."

. . . and his words of comfort to one crucified at his side . . .

"Tonight we will be in paradise."

Mary is inconsolable in her second verse, and Jesus continues, in the text from John's account, telling the "disciple whom

Jesus loved" to consider Mary his mother, and for Mary to consider the "disciple whom Jesus loved" as her son. At this moment in the cantata, Jesus and Mary express this last wish as a duet. I feel certain that this is the last time that Jesus would have been able to look upon his mother and appreciate her grief, offering her what protection he could.

The final words of Jesus emphasize his pain, anguish, and isolation. For me, these words also suggest his resignation to or acceptance of the will of God; perhaps they indicate his courageous acceptance of the inevitable consequence of Truth speaking to Power. I chose to set these final moments apart, with the text being sung in hushed tones, between moments of silence. Then, a rising call-and-response pattern between Jesus and the crowd builds as Jesus commits his spirit to God and dies uttering the words, "It is finished."

Call-and-response singing involves a leader singing a phrase and the chorus or congregation repeats the phrase or responds to it. I employed this as a sacred rhythm, where I imagine the crowd present at Golgotha to be rising and falling with every final word and breath of Jesus. Even as Jesus dies and commits his soul to the Father, there is a nobility evident, and the crowd responds with a "Hallelujah" and "Blessed is he who comes in the name of the Lord."

We are told by the Gospel writers that upon Jesus's last breath the skies darken, the earth shakes, and the temple curtain is rent in two. Musically we need to feel the crowd's deep awe and dread at the death of this extraordinary man. This moment is holy, even though it is a moment of great tragedy and sadness.

The final chord, sung by the choir, is discordant and dissonant as it swells, and then, like Jesus's life, is abruptly ended.

— A New Song —

But on the first day of the week, at early dawn, they came to the tomb, taking the spices that they had prepared. They found the stone rolled away from the tomb, but when they went in, they did not find the body. While they were perplexed about this, suddenly two men in dazzling clothes stood beside them. The women were terrified and bowed their faces to the ground, but the men said to them, "Why do you look for the living among the dead? He is not here, but has risen. Remember how he told you, while he was still in Galilee, that the Son of Man must be handed over to sinners, and be crucified, and on the third day rise again." (Luke 24:1–7)

A New Song

He is risen; why seek the living with the dead?
Why seek the living in the cold grave?

Where is my Lord? Where has he gone?
Where has he gone? Where is my Lord?
Why seek the living in the cold grave?

I waited patiently for the Lord,
He turned and heard my cry,
He raised me up from the pit of destruction,
He set my feet on stone, my gaze up on high.

He is risen; why seek the living with the dead?
Why seek the living in the cold grave?

Where is my Lord? Where has he gone?
Where has he gone? Where is my Lord?
Why seek the living in the cold grave?

He put a new song in my mouth,
    a hymn of praise to our God
Many will see and fear the Lord,
Many more will turn and trust the sound
Of a new song . . .

I have come to free the captives
To feed the hungry, clothe the naked
I have come to bring long-delayed justice to the poor!

Marcus

Growing up, I always thought of myself as a child-of-Easter as opposed to being a child-of-Christmas, I suppose; a flattering juxtaposition of the joy of receiving a risen Savior versus the joy of receiving gifts. Or maybe it was just the music, hearing Handel's "Hallelujah" chorus, the greatest of all Easter musical expressions. Perhaps it was waking up and hearing my mother or father say, "Christ is risen," and responding "He is risen indeed!" Any way you look at it, I have always loved Easter: sunrise service, Easter egg hunt, the whole thing!

I have also always found it fleeting. When the rush of Easter day is past, we return to our normal lives, quickly forgetting the purpose and hopefulness of Easter morning, missing the richness of its fifty-day season. A professor of mine at Vanderbilt Divinity School (many years ago, I took a few courses there and met my future wife), Dr. Peter Hodgson, used to reflect on his theory of "spiraling forms of liberation." That is, life is like the double helix of a DNA strand with most of our lives drawn inward to the mundane, the mean, and the absurd. Only occasionally do we spiral outward and touch the divine, finding illumination and meaning! This seems an apt description of most of our spiritual lives—if we even have a spiritual life—but it is a somewhat depressing thought.

Through working on *The Passion* I have found that the child-of-Lent was more likely to sustain strength through the example of Christ than the child-of-Easter. It is almost impossible to fully grasp the transcendent Christ emerging from the tomb and integrate that wondrous image into the dailyness of our lives. (The great singer Pearl Bailey once said that the problem with life was that it was just so daily!) If this is true in the comfortable postmodern Western world in which most of us live, imagine how much more important it is to the majority of the world's population living with more depravation, more hunger, more violence, and more sorrow than we can comprehend.

The image of the Easter Christ is a kind of "quick fix" for many of us Christians, where the Lenten Christ is too painful, too "real" at times for our full reflection and attention. The Lenten Christ knows the fulfillment and joy of entering the Holy City, greeted by countless famished souls, hungry for a word of truth and redemption—a word of compassion. He also knows what it is to weep at the entrance to the city and to contemplate the hardship and brutality ahead. The Lenten Christ knows what it is to sit and share a meal with close friends, to have fellowship, to love; but the Lenten Christ also knows what it is to see a friend "turn," finding himself betrayed, and turned over to enemies. We understand, in our humanity, what it is to want to "pass this cup from my lips," and we feel Jesus's strength in ultimately accepting "Your will and not mine." We have been there; we have lived all of this. The Lenten Christ takes all the world can throw at him and says in response, "Forgive them, they know not what they do"; as the light fades on his mortal life, the Lenten Christ reaches out to comfort those he loves, making sure one of his friends looks after his mother after he is gone.

In other words, the Lenten Christ makes for better theater! It is almost impossible to find the music for the mind of a divine child, or to express the voice of a transcendent being, risen from the dead; however, there is music for someone who asks for companionship on a dark night of the soul, knowing that enemies are about to descend upon him. There is certainly music for a man who, knowing his time on earth is short, asks those dear to him to remember how and why he loved them so much.

Still, having grown up in the faith, it felt strange to leave Jesus in the tomb. I was commissioned to create a piece for Palm Sunday, and not Easter Sunday, but I wanted to compose an expression of the joy of the Risen Lord.

I am often led by the seemingly coincidental comment or observation. So it was that as my good friend Father Charlie Stroebel and I were discussing *The Passion* one night on our porch, I told him that I wanted to write an Easter piece even though the cantata focused on the Palm Sunday liturgy. I told him I didn't know how to write about such an audacious claim as the waking of the dead, the raising of our Lord.

Without directly speaking to my frustration over a potential Easter piece, Charlie mentioned that on a trip to Jerusalem, his guide had suggested that before Jesus was crucified, the Romans might have put him in a pit; that the Romans used to place the condemned in deeply dug holes in the ground the night before their execution so that they might consider their coming ordeal beneath the stars, naked in the evening chill. The Romans had a genius for cruelty.

This led me to one of my favorite Psalms:

> I waited patiently for the Lord; he inclined to me and heard my cry. He drew me up from the desolate pit, out of the miry bog, and set my feet upon rock, making my steps secure. He put a new song in my mouth, a song of praise to our God. Many will see and fear, and put their trust in the Lord. (Psalm 40:1–3)

This is a text that expresses the joy of freedom, and "freedom" in many ways is how I understand resurrection. I see resurrection as the ongoing work of love in the world, the corporal acts of mercy: to feed the hungry, give drink to the thirsty, shelter the homeless, visit the sick and the prisoner, give alms to the poor, and bury the dead. I also see resurrection as the arc of history bending toward justice, as Martin Luther King reminded us.

I remember in the mid-1980s traveling to Botswana for the summer to visit my folks who were stationed in Gaborone, my dad the director of the USAID program (Agency For International Development). In those days, the only international airport was in Johannesburg, South Africa, and South Africa was still in the throes of apartheid. I can still see the long line of blacks being herded through the gates of Soweto, the barbed-wire enclosed sprawling shanty city on the edge of town, at curfew. I remember the "whites only" signs on bathrooms and water fountains, and the feeling that somehow, just by standing there and witnessing the suffering of others, I was complicit. Even though I was just trying to find a bus to take me north to Botswana, somehow, I was complicit.

Now, many years later, Becca and I and our community at St. Augustine's Chapel on the Vanderbilt campus have had the opportunity to be in relationship with the Holy Cross Hospice just outside of Gaborone, a beautiful ministry to those in the poorest part of the thriving city, offering palliative care for those afflicted with HIV/AIDs and also caring for those orphaned by this scourge. We have also sent young leaders to live and work at the hospice, and in doing so, have become a community together. In traveling to Botswana and elsewhere in sub-Saharan Africa,

I have found myself spending time in South Africa, and though there is still great inequity and challenges—clearly, hope has been resurrected! The life of Nelson Mandela and the work of forgiveness and reconciliation is a miracle in our times. Obviously there is still work to do in South Africa, as well as in our own racially divided nation, but we must raise up "resurrection" where we behold it and say, "Hallelujah!"

I love the term "new song" from the psalm, and feel that this is what anyone writing liturgical music should strive for; that is, to offer a new song or a new musical reflection on these foundational stories and ancient texts, songs and writings that are anything but "new." Still, even as we retell the stories, reread the verses, sing again the beloved hymns of our youth, we desire new artistic expressions of our passion for God, our passion for Jesus. I wanted to end this cantata with a joyful gospel-music interpretation of these verses of Psalm 40. How many times has this text been read or sung, no one knows. As Ecclesiastes 1:7 says, "All streams run to the sea, but the sea is not full; to the place where the streams flow, there they continue to flow."

It is common practice for me to drive around in my truck singing to myself, waiting on the muse and musical inspiration. This particular day, I kept singing the words, "He is risen, why seek the living with the dead?" the admonition of the angel to the women who had come to the tomb three days after Jesus's crucifixion to anoint his body. As I sang the baritone opening, I found myself stomping with my foot on the brake pad, causing the truck to jolt "in time," and hitting the steering wheel with one hand. It's a wonder I didn't crash. I began to imagine a choir clapping and foot stomping in a driving rhythm. Then other voices occurred to me as well, and I found it necessary to pull off the road, and record my ideas into my phone.

In writing this cantata, I humbly offer my own musical meditation on Lent, on the suffering and sacrifice of our Lord. In writing *The Passion* and having the opportunity to delve deeply into the various traditions surrounding Jesus's final days, his suffering and resurrection, I found that I have a renewed "passion" for this faith of ours. I found that I still love the stories of Jesus, and still love Jesus.

Again and again, he is risen!

Becca

As Marcus's joyful conclusion to *The Passion* opens, the first thing I notice is Mary Magdalene's voice singing, "Where is my Lord?" She is the constant fixture in all the resurrection narratives across the four Gospels. The other characters change, but she is always there with her spices, early in the morning, seeking to find her Lord. It is as if the Lord lingers for her and that her love and gratitude are so powerful that she is determined to find him, even as the disciples are huddled in a room afraid of their own fate. The music, the poetry, the joy and longing all remind me of a dance. At the end of this cantata and all our contemplation of the Passion, we need to just dance.

We all do a dance with mortality. It's a pas de deux with our creator. Our dance with mortality goes something like this: first we turn our backs and then we come round right with a graceful bow toward the eternal. There we genuflect and hold grief and hope in harmony. Sometimes the movements look fearful and heavy-laden, when in reality they are courageous and tender. We have all done the dance. We move in fear, weep at gravesides, and lift our eyes for signs. There are signs all around us, drawing us to make resurrection part of our dance.

Our own mortality and the mortality of everyone we love is hard to fathom; it makes sense that it feels more like a dance to us than a conversation. We share a powerful fear that grief will be our undoing. Kissing someone we love good-bye and kissing hello a new life is almost too much for our heart to bear in real time. Yet we move through them both in a dance we inherited from those who loved us. We don't have words or even rational thoughts. We feel the love and hope deep in our bones; death is not the end of our dance.

No one does the dance with more grace than Mary Magdalene. Our Easter story in John begins with her full of grief, setting out while it is still dark to anoint Jesus's body. We can hear the quiet as she enters the garden with spices and oils. I wonder if Magdalene, burdened with leadership and love, looked down long enough to consider the lilies as they bore a regal witness to hope. I wonder if the path she took smelled rich and offered her hope as she prepared to face the stone. I wonder if she saw the fragrant flowers as a sign that even in the midst of death, love was rising. I wonder then if she remembered Jesus's words as he led them on their first mission, "Don't worry about your life." "Seek the kingdom, and all else will be added unto you" (Matthew 6:26–28). She must have been filled with grief with the scene of the crucifixion still fresh in her memory. She must have felt her aloneness and realized the possibility of her own death, walking toward the guards surrounding Jesus's sealed tomb.

It is when she sees the stone rolled away that the resurrection dance begins. First she runs from the tomb for help, then Peter and John race toward the tomb, trying to understand what they are witnessing. Peter and John then turn back, and then Mary Magdalene, weeping, turns toward the empty tomb and bows gracefully to look closer into the tomb. She sees the angels and realizes she isn't alone, and asks for her Lord. Finally, turning again, she hears the voice of her Lord who has lingered at the tomb for her, "Mary!" For a moment, she dances with eternity. We, like Mary, have been called by name and are God's own forever. We, like Mary, can weep and call like timeless poets, "Come, my Joy, my Love, my Heart" and move with our risen Lord in a dance that takes us by surprise.

Sometimes we dance close to mortality. I have preached in Ecuador on Ash Wednesday during a drought and could taste the dust of the land in my mouth. It was as clear to me as it had ever been that we are truly dust, and that is why there is no difference—male or female, Ecuadorean or American, rich or poor; we are dust, and to dust we shall return. There was no bitterness in the taste for me. It was just laden with gratitude. Gratitude for all the love shared along the way. When the service concluded, I walked outside the small church where eight-foot speakers had been set up while we were marking our heads with ashes. Those speakers started bellowing out dance music as the teachers and students of the school where we work every year changed into an array of dancing costumes. Three hundred people gathered around the basketball court, clapping and dancing. The kindergarten teacher, dressed in a clown outfit of rags with fresh ashes still adorning her forehead, came out with all the children to wild applause. Through teary eyes and laughter I witnessed one of the most beautiful dances I have ever seen. She was like Mary herself, fearlessly bending into the empty tomb, and then turning round and round because life and hope are stronger. I want us to keep moving in hope while the ashes are fresh on our foreheads. Easter preaches, "Dance: love is more powerful than fear, stronger than the grave, and older than grief."

Love always finds a way to bloom and make our hearts dance—in spinning circles on Ash Wednesday, in the dance we do with our mortality, and with the new life we find on Easter mornings when we can sing with Jesus and join in on the psalmist's happy song,

> He put a new song in my mouth,
> a song of praise to our God.
> Many will see and fear,
> and put their trust in the Lord.
> Happy are those who make
> the Lord their trust[13]

singing by our gravesides.

— —

---

13. Psalm 40:3–4

The invitation and reflection for our Easter song is to remember the dance. To remember when you have participated in that dance in your life and when you have been uplifted by resurrection. Share a story of hope. Give thanks for all the ways love is resurrected in you and through you. Call upon the Lord and seek him in the places you fear or that feel desolate . . . look again.

The message of *The Passion* in the good news of resurrection is that love lives. This is the living word of God. This cantata is meant to send us out to love the world again and to be with the living with our whole hearts. To go love the world renewed by the power of the Holy Spirit, and then to make our way back to dust, back to our creator, still making our song, "Alleluia, Alleluia, Alleluia."